Granite

Susan Butcher and David Monson

Illustrated by Sarah Douglas

Trail Breaker Kennel
P.O. Box 60249
Fairbanks, Alaska 99706

www.susanbutcher.com

To all the dogs who preceded Granite,
to his teammates who made his victories possible,
and to all who follow in his paw prints.

Every year a sled dog race crosses the frozen wilderness of Alaska. It is called the Iditarod. It starts in Anchorage and crosses three mountain ranges, two river valleys and the frozen Bering Sea to end over a 1,000 miles later in Nome. The race honors the dogs and mushers who hauled mail, supplies, and life-saving medicine through the Alaska winters 100 years ago. One dog in the Iditarod race came to epitomize the strength, courage, and intelligence of those dogs long ago: **Granite.**

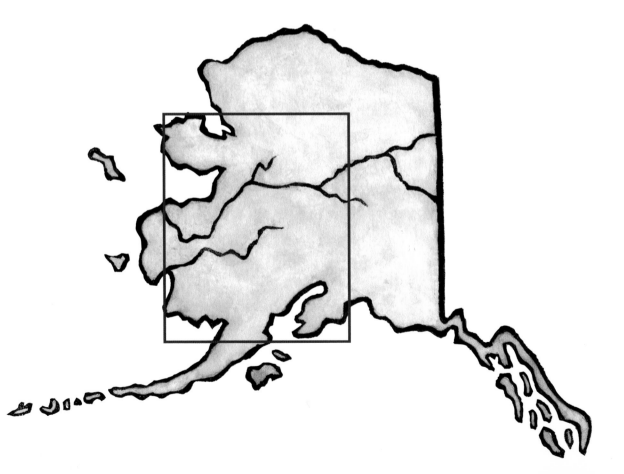

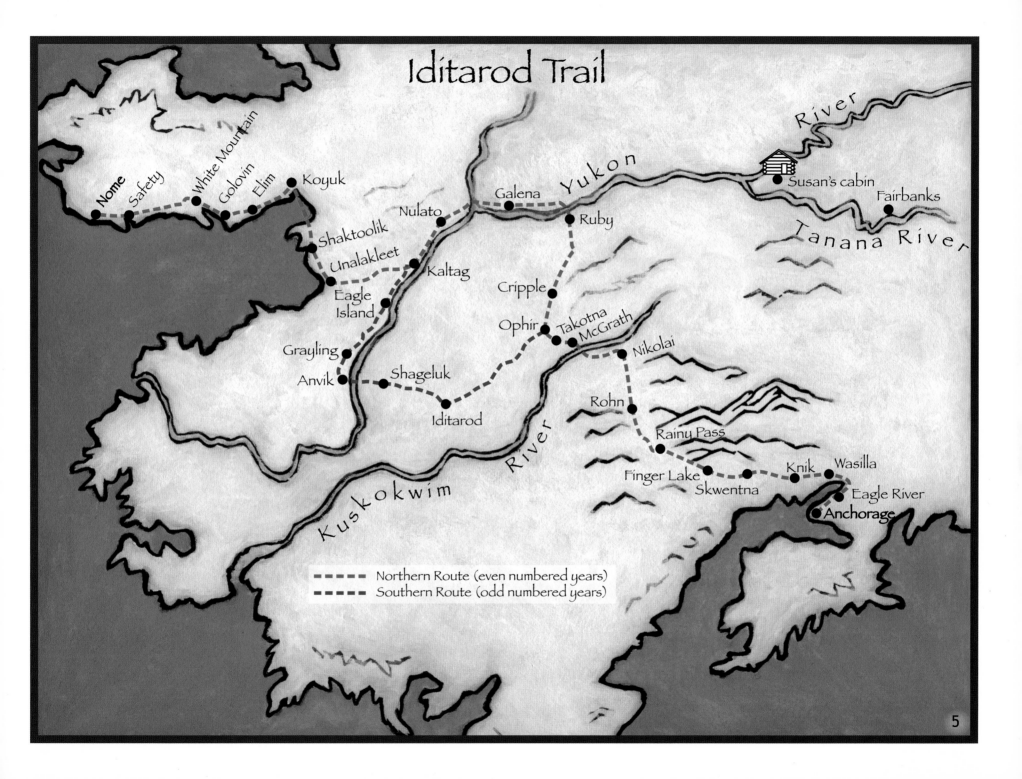

Iditarod Trail

Nome
Safety
White Mountain
Golovin
Elim
Koyuk

Shaktoolik
Nulato
Galena
Ruby

Unalakleet
Kaltag

Eagle Island
Cripple

Grayling
Ophir
Takotna
McGrath

Anvik
Shageluk
Nikolai

Iditarod
Rohn

Rainy Pass

Finger Lake
Knik
Wasilla
Skwentna
Eagle River
Anchorage

River
Yukon
Tanana River
Fairbanks
Susan's cabin
Kuskokwim
River

Northern Route (even numbered years)
Southern Route (odd numbered years)

Susan Butcher lived alone in the Alaska wilderness with her sled dogs. Her home was a little log cabin. Susan was a musher, so in the winter she traveled across the snow-covered trails on a dog sled. The dogs loved pulling her sled and she loved them in return.

One spring day while Susan was feeding her dogs, she heard a familiar sound. Puppies were being born. Quietly, she walked over to the barn. Listening at the door, she heard cooing. Slowly she looked inside, and there on a cozy bed of straw were five newborn pups. Their mother gently nuzzled them and cleaned each one with her tongue as they lay curled up next to her. All the pups were shiny, fat, and healthy—except for one. His fur was dull, he had knock-knees, and he let the others push him away from their mother.

Susan loved the puppies and was proud of each one. She was always showing them off to other mushers who visited. Again and again, the visitors would say they all looked great, except for the timid one. They said that he would never become a real sled dog and she should give him away to someone as a pet. But Susan believed in him, so she gave him a strong name: Granite.

When the pups were old enough, she started taking them on daily walks in the woods. Susan and the puppies developed a close bond. Susan watched Granite and was impressed by his intelligence. He always knew where he was because he remembered the trails they had taken before. Even when they went somewhere new, he could find his way home alone while his brothers and sisters closely followed Susan so they would not get lost. Every evening they ran together to develop his strength. She was sure that someday he would race on her team.

Granite grew to be a fifty-eight-pound, deep-chested, fast dog. He overcame his knock-kneed legs with a powerful stride. He pulled the sled better than the others, and his confidence grew. He learned to lead the team. Leaders need to be able to guide the team over rough trails, find the way when they are lost, and run fast. Granite did all three. After years of work, Granite became the main lead dog of Susan's racing team.

At the start of his first Iditarod, Granite seemed to sense it was a race. He stood in front of the team with his head held high, waiting for the command to go. Finally the race started and Granite charged down the trail. Susan was amazed by him. They stopped often to eat and rest. When it was time to go again Granite would be the first to jump to his feet, barking and prancing, anxious to head down the trail. 13

Soon they were leading the race. One night when they crested a small hill, there in the trail ahead of them stood an angry moose. Susan stopped the team to let the moose get away, but it didn't run. Instead it charged into the team, kicking and stomping. Granite lunged at the moose, trying to protect his teammates, but the moose kicked him and he flew against a tree.

When the attack was over, Susan saw the damage the moose had done. She gently cared for her injured teammates before deciding that for the good of her beloved dogs, they should leave their dream of winning behind. They withdrew from the race. She took her bruised and battered team home but promised the dogs that next year, they would win.

People doubted Susan and Granite. They often said, "Susan will never win the Iditarod because she babies her dogs." Susan didn't listen to them and continued to care for her dogs as she always had.

It was a long, hard year. Susan and the dogs worked tirelessly to recover. In the fall Susan and her dogs started running every day, training for the race.

One day on a short run Susan saw Granite falter. She stopped the team and rushed to him. It was quickly clear to her something was wrong. Granite tried but he could not get to his feet. Granite's temperature was soaring, his heart was racing, and he was fading fast. Granite needed help, but help was far away. She bundled him up and they flew to a veterinary hospital.

The doctor held little hope for his recovery. Susan set up a cot next to Granite and stayed with him day and night, petting him and willing him to live. Granite lived, but the veterinarian gently told Susan he would never race again. The illness had damaged his heart.

19

When Granite was able they flew back home. Susan and the dogs continued to train, while Granite rested in the cabin, watching the leaves turn colors and slowly fall. Before the snow came, the dogs pulled Susan on a four-wheeled cart to get stronger. Granite cried and howled every time the team left him behind. He was determined to get better.

Slowly but surely Granite showed improvement. The veterinarian told Susan Granite could start running loose with the puppies.

As winter came, Granite was back in the team but only training with young dogs on shorter runs. Meanwhile, the main racing team was running many long miles under the northern lights. Still every night after Susan returned, Granite would sleep on her bed. Gradually his strength returned.

The doctor was amazed at his progress. As a test of his recovery, Susan let him run a short race with the young dogs. Granite proved he was healthy by leading that team to victory. His determination, drive, and strength convinced Susan he could race the Iditarod again. But had his endurance come back? Could he finish the 1,000-mile race?

The Iditarod started in early March. Granite was at the starting line, leading her team again. To win they had to beat last year's champion. Day after day the two teams raced, always close to each other. The trail turned out to be tough for Susan and her team. The sled broke, and many times they were lost. But Granite never faltered.

Near the end of the race, the two teams were only seventeen seconds apart. Susan and Granite were ahead, but suddenly the other team passed them and pulled away. Susan thought, "well, I guess second place is okay." Then she looked at the dogs working so hard and remembered her promise to them: "this is our year to win." She called out to Granite and he responded. They charged by the other team. Again they had a small lead in the race.

As they left an Eskimo village 100 miles from the finish line in Nome, a furious storm hit. Susan often could not see the trail, but Granite kept on going. Finally the snow was blowing across the ground so thick Susan couldn't even see Granite at the front of the team.

Granite had to find the trail on his own. From time to time he would get lost, so Susan would lean into the wind and walk up to the front of the team to help him regain the trail. Together they went on.

As the storm raged, Susan's arms were becoming frozen. She could barely hang on to the sled. They had to get to shelter soon. Granite saw that Susan needed his help. Finally Susan couldn't move at all. Her arms were hurting so badly that she was beginning to lose hope, but Granite kept forging ahead. He knew Susan was in trouble, and it was up to him to get them through. The other dogs were following his lead. If he quit, they would too, and all would be lost. He kept going, step after step, on through the blizzard. Susan was quiet and hunched over the sled. This was it.

Suddenly they saw dim lights from the next checkpoint. They had made it through the blizzard.

Susan and the team rested there, eating hot meals throughout the stormy night. In the morning they ran the last 76 miles to Nome and won the Iditarod. All of the other teams in the race had been turned back by the storm and did not finish until eighteen hours later. Susan and Granite had done it. They had won the Iditarod and set a new record time.

The next two years they won again with Granite proudly leading the team. With Susan's love and Granite's strength they had become unstoppable. Now those same people who had not believed in them said, "It's no wonder they win the race because she takes the best care of her dogs and they take care of her."

Epilogue

Granite won every race he entered at least once. In 1988, he became the only lead dog ever to win the Iditarod three times in a row. Granite retired from racing after Susan's fourth Iditarod victory. He traveled extensively with Susan and even went to the White House to visit the president. But his favorite place was always their cabin in the wilderness, where he watched the puppy teams head down the trails on their own adventures. Granite lived seventeen and a half years and died in Susan's arms.

2nd edition copyright © 2008 Trail Breaker Kennel
All rights reserved.

Trail Breaker Kennel
5880 Airport Industrial Road
Fairbanks, Alaska 99709   USA
books@susanbutcher.com
www.susanbutcher.com

ISBN: 978-0-9754029-2-4 (cloth)
        978-0-9754029-3-1 (paper)

The Elmer E. Rasmuson Library cataloged the first edition as:
Butcher, Susan.
Granite / Susan Butcher and David Monson ; illustrated by Sarah Douglas.
    Fairbanks, Alaska : Trail Breaker Kennel, 2007.
    p. cm.
ISBN: 978-0-9754029-1-7 (hbk.)
ISBN: 978-0-9754029-0-0 (pbk.)
ISBN: 978-0-9754029-2-4 (special cloth ed.)

1. Granite (Sled dog)—Juvenile literature. 2. Sled dogs—Alaska—Juvenile
literature. 3. Dogsledding—Alaska—Juvenile literature. 4. Sled dog racing—Alaska—Juvenile literature. 5. Iditarod (Race)—Juvenile literature.
I. Monson, David, 1952-. II. Douglas, Sarah Nairn. III. Title.

SF428.7.B88 2007

Printed by Samhwa Printing Co., Ltd., Seoul, Korea.

Third printing January, 2009

Artwork by Sarah Douglas (www.sarahdouglas.com)
Book design and layout by Sue Mitchell, Inkworks

Granite's statue stands in front of the Susan Butcher Family Center at Providence Hospital in Anchorage, Alaska. The center is dedicated to providing support and comfort to children who have parents or loved ones with cancer.